Kiara Wilson

MISTAKES ARE HOW I LEARN

Tamara had big dreams.
But every time she would fail
And was forced to take a step back,
Tamara would give up and bail.

Her mistakes would infuriate her
And make her so mad.
Perfection is what she sought.
To her, messing up was bad.

Her parents tried to comfort her.
"Mistakes are how we learn.
That is how we grow
With each twist and turn."

So, Tamara set goals
To conquer one day.
I will let a growth mindset
Lead the way."

Even when life
Makes me fret,
I won't say, "I can't do this."
I'll say "I can't do this, yet!"

So Tamara tried out
For the gymnastics team,
But she wasn't selected.
Did this shatter her dream?

She just said, "There's next year.
I'll just take it steady,
And practice each day
Until I am ready."

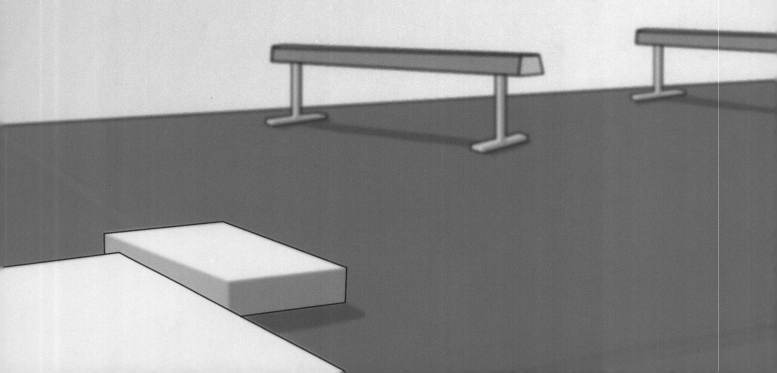

We all make mistakes,
And sometimes we fail,
But each setback's a lesson
That we need to nail.

At school in a math test,
She received a "C".
So Tamara studied harder,
And the next test scored a "B."

All successful people
Struggle sometimes.
They reach within
To find the strength inside.

When obstacles come up,
They rise to the occasion
And become more determined
To find their motivation.

Tamara learned to say,
"All my dreams will come true,
If I have a growth mindset
In all that I do."

So even when something
Seems tough at first glance,
Just keep on pushing.
You'll soon get your chance.

Mistakes are how I learn.
I will get there soon.
I'll keep dreaming big
Even if it's flying to the moon.

Dear reader,

Thank you for picking up my book, "Mistakes Are How I Learn." I have a passion for helping others in all that they do! I am a living breathing testament of living life with doubt and fear. It wasn't until I was well in my 30s that it dawned on me, it was okay not to be perfect. I hope my books inspire the next generation to reach within and aim high.

I would be so appreciative if you left a review for my book. Every review counts.

With love,
Kiara

Printed in the USA
CPSIA information can be obtained
at www.ICGtesting.com
LVHW072139231023

761891LV00017B/270